ACADEMIC AND
LEGAL DEPOSIT LIBRARIES

ACADEMIC AND
LEGAL DEPOSIT LIBRARIES

AN EXAMINATION GUIDEBOOK

BY DONALD DAVINSON FLA

SENIOR LECTURER LEEDS SCHOOL OF LIBRARIANSHIP

CLIVE BINGLEY  LONDON

FIRST PUBLISHED 1965 BY CLIVE BINGLEY LTD
16 PEMBRIDGE ROAD LONDON W 11
SET IN LINOTYPE 10 ON 12 POINT BASKERVILLE
AND PRINTED IN GREAT BRITAIN
BY THE CENTRAL PRESS (ABERDEEN) LTD

CONTENTS

INTRODUCTION

THE *Examination guides* are a new concept in texts for librarianship studies. They are a series of short books designed to cater specifically for the Library Association final part II examination. They follow exactly the pattern laid down in the official syllabus. They are intended for use both within the framework of a library school course and also for students studying privately, especially those who need a ' key ' guide for speedy pre-examination revision.

Within the library school it is envisaged that the *guides* may be used by tutors as a supplement to formal lecture programmes and as a means of providing students with a guiding framework for each course. Specifications for essays, reports and drafts to be submitted for a tutor's consideration can be taken from the *guides* without the need for comprehensive lecturing which might reduce the likelihood of original, free thinking work.

The intelligent library student should find the *guides* invaluable companions in final revision work. The authors have analysed each subject and drawn attention to the key points in summary form, backed up with carefully selected readings to provide amplification. Thus any of the topics can be followed up directly in detail. For a student already familiar with the syllabus the *guides* provide both a method for revision and a fresh approach to their subjects.

Part time and private study students should not regard the *guides* as a substitute for wider and more detailed reading. Their prime function is to enable the student to recognise the key features in each subject. Too often students with little or no tutorial guidance fail to obtain a proper perspective and may spend a disproportionate amount of time on comparatively minor topics.

The *Examination guides* series is edited by Donald Davinson FLA, senior lecturer at the Leeds school of librarianship. Other *guides* in course of preparation are *Public library administration* by George Jefferson FLA, *Theory of classification* by Keith Davison FLA, *Theory of cataloguing* by P J Quigg FLA, *Practical cata-*

7

loguing by W Dent FLA, *Special libraries and information bureaux* by H R Astall ALA, *Library service for young people* by Stella Pinches ALA and *Dissemination of information* by T D Wilson FLA and J Stephenson FLA. Further titles in the series will include *Bibliography* and other optional papers from the final part II examination syllabus, and will also cover parts of the newly introduced graduate syllabus. Coverage of certain subjects from the final part II list C syllabus is also planned.

CHAPTER ONE
HISTORY AND FUNCTIONS

THE NATIONAL LIBRARY

STUDENTS' first thoughts will probably be of the British Museum, Bibliothèque Nationale and the Library of Congress, and after this of the Scottish and Welsh National Libraries. An appreciation of the role of these libraries is important. To confine study to these libraries only would be a too limiting background, for there are other countries in which the role of the national library is more precisely defined and more fully integrated into the national system of libraries.

The developing countries show some of the most interesting thinking on the development of a system of libraries around a national library and the provision of a comprehensive advisory and information service. The opportunity which such libraries have had to plan ' from the ground up ' is one which librarians in in the older countries must envy. In spite of inadequacies of stock and trained staff, several recently established national libraries have interesting prospects. Many newer foundations were launched by librarians from the older countries working as seconded advisers.

The part played by UNESCO in promoting the growth of national libraries since 1945 should be appreciated. Reports of their work programmes are a regular feature in UNESCO *Bulletin for libraries*. The scope of the activities of national libraries in developing countries is illustrated by the reports of the ' Regional seminar on the development of national libraries in Asia and the Pacific area ' UNESCO *Bulletin for libraries* 18 (14) July-August 1964.

THE FUNCTIONS OF NATIONAL LIBRARIES

These are summarised on page 151 of the UNESCO *Bulletin* noted above.

1 To provide leadership among the nation's libraries.
2 To serve as a permanent depository for all publications deposited in the country.

3 To acquire other types of material.
4 To provide bibliographical services.
5 To serve as a co-ordinating centre for co-operative activities.
6 To provide services to government.

The role of the national library was thoroughly examined at a UNESCO symposium on national libraries in Europe in September 1958. *National libraries: their problems and prospects* (UNESCO 1960) presents the papers given. Summaries of the symposium were given in *Libri* 9 (4) 1959, 273-307 and in UNESCO *Bulletin* 13 (1) Jan 1959 1-4. Other readings are Arundel Esdaile ' The great libraries of the world and their functions' *Library review* (94) summer 1950 344-349 and F C Francis ' The contribution of the national library to the modern outlook on library services' ASLIB *Proceedings* 10 (11) November 1958 267-275. *National libraries* (Library Association 1963) is extracts from an LA University and Research Section conference 1963.

The extent to which national libraries mentioned in the opening paragraph carry out the six listed functions should be examined. It is interesting to consider the effect, for good or ill, of individual personalities on the development of these libraries, Panizzi at the British Museum, Putnam at the Library of Congress, Ballinger at the National Library of Wales, Van Praet at the BN amongst others. Note that many European national libraries have developed out of the Royal Library and, indeed, still are ' the Royal' in some cases *eg* Denmark, Belgium. The Sovereign's interest in the library is sometimes a significant factor in its development.

The Lenin Library in Moscow must not be ignored. An article indicating its great degree of integration into the national system is I Kondakov ' The Centenary of the Lenin State Library' UNESCO *Bulletin* 17 (1) Jan-Feb 1963 25-26: Jacob Miller's ' The Lenin Library' *Library review* (137) spring 1961 26-29 is a more generalised account of the service given. The collections are described in an article in *Times literary supplement* (3057) 29 June 1962, 484.

A starting point for the study of national libraries is *National libraries of the world* (Library Association 1957) the second edition of A Esdaile's work by F J Hill.

THE BRITISH MUSEUM LIBRARY

Nowhere is the truth of the historian's warning that it is unwise to ascribe one effect to one cause more clearly seen than in the study of the growth of the basic collections which formed the British Museum in 1753. Raymond Irwin's article ' The approach to a national library in England ' *Library Association record* 64 (3) March 1962 81-93 examines the various streams which merged to form the core of the national library and museum. Sir Hans Sloane's material contributed to both elements but there were other fine basic collections including those of the Harleys, Cotton and a little later, the Royal Library. The study of the British Museum library must begin, as Irwin does, with the genesis of these and other collections.

The effects of the dissolution of the monasteries, which released the materials which ultimately found their way into the BM by way of the Cotton and Harley collections, and others, need attention. The growth of the collections and of the library can be traced through Arundel Esdaile *The British Museum library* (Allen and Unwin 1946). Further information can be had from F J Hill ' The British Museum library' *Library world* 62 (726) December 1960 129-135 to which is appended a further list of readings. The discussions engendered by the passage of the bill which became the British Museum Act 1963 need consideration. The library is to be re-housed and will provide improved reader services and reader space. Some subject division will be introduced and also a closed circuit television and teleprinter link with the National Reference Library for Science and Invention. It is anticipated that present plans will be sufficient for 50-100 years. The re-organisation proposals were reported in *Bookseller* 28 April 1962 and *British Museum quarterly* 25 (3-4) June 1962 55-60.

A survey of the BM must include study of its greatest librarian, Antonio Panizzi (1797-1879). An Italian exiled in 1822, he taught in Liverpool and London, was appointed an assistant keeper at BM 1831, had a rapid rise to keeper of Printed Books 1837, becoming finally principal librarian 1856-1866. Lasting influence seen in BM code of cataloguing rules, in the great catalogue of 1880-1905, increased financial recognition of BM staff and his broad concept of book selection policy. His greatest single asset was his ability to make powerful friends and use them. An objective study must not be blind to his faults—tactlessness, overbearing manner, inconsistent staff management, ill temper—the effects not always good for BM.

The BM should not be under rated. Its inadequacies must be balanced against its strengths, some of which are indicated by an interesting comparison of the BM and L of C printed catalogues by A H Chaplin ' Statistical comparison of the British Museum and Library of Congress catalogues ' *Journal of documentation* 15 (1) March 1959 68. The effects of the re-alignments consequent upon the formation of the National Reference Library for Science and Invention should be noted. A good current source of information is the BM trustees' *The British Museum: a guide to its public services.*

THE LIBRARY OF CONGRESS

Established 1800, Congress previously using Franklin's Library Company of Philadelphia. Library destroyed 1814, re-established under first full time librarian, George Watterson, with 6,000 volumes of President Jefferson's library. In 1816 liberal interpretation of the rules opened library to scholars generally. Librarian appointment frequent cause of political friction in the nineteenth century. Ainsworth Spofford librarian 1864-1897. Period of great growth into national research collection culminating in new buildings to last a century. Herbert Putnam (1861-1955) appointed librarian 1899 after political row. Appointment a triumph for the ALA. Putnam as ex-librarian of Boston public library is first ' career ' librarian. During period of office to 1939 collections increased tenfold. Spofford's buildings full after only 20 years. Putnam added two huge stacks and an annexe larger than the whole of the rest.

Putman was a remarkably able, inspired leader and fearless delegator to chosen subordinates. Every task he set himself was achieved in his lifetime. His printed card project helped to make the L of C the centre of American librarianship. The L of C classification and the consultants and subject specialists were other notable features of his tenure of office.

McLeish (1939-1944) was a successful reversion to a non-librarian. Farmington Plan first tentatively proposed at one of his advisory committees. Dr Luther Evans (1944-1953) was promoted from chief assistantship then left to become Director-General of UNESCO. The eleventh Librarian of Congress is the first library school graduate to hold the appointment, L Quincey Mumford.

The L of C is currently the subject of discussion—should it become the national library in fact as well as by tradition? ' Pyramid or volcano?' by Paul Dunkin *Library journal* 88 (1) Jan 1st 1963 51-57 summarises a dialogue between L Q Mumford and D J Bryant on this question.

Services to the national library system include the *National union catalog*, subject headings lists and codes of cataloguing rules, a classification scheme, participation in inter-library cooperation, printed catalogue cards and the highly significant books for the blind scheme. Another useful reading is Elizabeth E Hamer's ' Library of Congress: an introduction to everybody's library' *Library journal* 90 (1) Jan 1st 1965.

LA BIBLIOTHÈQUE NATIONALE

Began as Royal Library, open to students and French monarchs, almost without exception, interested in its development. Had many able librarians, Bude, Colbert, the Bignon family and Van Praet. Praet continued after the revolution when library declared a national institution. Had first pick of suppressed monasteries and noble houses, collected in the *depôts littéraires*. Middle of the nineteenth century funds inadequate, revived briefly under De Lisle 1874-1907, waned after 1914 and again revived briefly in the late 1920's. During the inter-war years considerable modernisation of methods and buildings. *Réunion de bibliothèques nationales de Paris* formed 1926 and union catalogues of their holdings begun. Author catalogue (begun 1897) accelerated and bibliographic services designed to make the BN the focus of the national library system.

The war again reduced BN potency and produced serious arrears of work. Purchase funds were, until recently, never more than barely adequate, but despite all the BN has achieved some remarkable standards, notably in the quality of its senior staff and of the manuscript collections.

NATIONAL LIBRARY OF SCOTLAND

Grew out of the Faculty of Advocates Library founded 1682 and taken over by the government in 1925 (see National Library of Scotland Act 1925). History and growth of the collections recorded in Esdaile and Hill and *Times literary supplement,* 28th August 1953. Its policy is to provide a Scottish collection primarily, and then a general research collection of high international repute biased in favour of the humanities. Two departments, Printed Books and Manuscripts, stock more than one and a half million volumes. New buildings opened in 1955.

National Eisteddfod in 1873 proposed formation—collections begun. Royal Charter 1907, librarian appointed 1929 (John Ballinger who found a strong nucleus based on Sir John Williams' collection. Permanent buildings begun 1911, central block finished 1955. Three departments, printed books, manuscripts, prints and drawings. Fine collections of Irish and Scots Gaelic, Manx, Cornish, Breton and Basque literature. Excellent work done on very small funds. First British library to be classified by Library of Congress scheme. Produces *Bibliotheca celtica*. Besides Esdaile and Hill an article in *Times literary supplement* July 10th 1953 and E D Jones The National Library of Wales' *Library world* 62 (728) February 1961 177-181 are the best summaries of the origins of the library, other than the library's own pamphlet published in 1962 *The National Library of Wales a brief summary of its history and its activities* and the annual reports.

NATIONAL LIBRARY FUNCTIONS COMPARED
The ideal sees the national library as the focus of a country's libraries, guiding, inspiring and experimenting, taking the lead in co-operation nationally and internationally, producing basic bibliography and being the central clearing house for bibliographic information through a national bibliographic centre. (See also *Access to information*: *a national bibliographical service* LA 1965, also in *Library Association record* 67 (4) April 1965 131-2.)

National libraries in Britain are aside from the national library system and exist virtually as separate entities, compared with the services given by many foreign national libraries. *Bibliotheca celtica* is an example of the basic bibliography function, but there has been little direct service to government, little innovation in recent years influencing other libraries. Virtually no cross fertilisation of ideas through staff movements, in or out.

The Library of Congress provides many of the services but only incidentally to its main purpose and, by strict definition, it is not a national library. The Lenin Library provides bibliographic clearing house facilities and exchange services, lends from its own stock, has drawn up a widely used classification scheme and houses a large library school. The BN is the centre for international exchanges, provides bibliographic services and a scheme of inter library co-operation.

Newly established national libraries have greater chance of becoming the centre of a national library system, and frequently do so through the creation of a national bibliographic centre (see Knud Larsen *National bibliographic services,* UNESCO 1955). In western Europe some of the smaller national libraries are strongly integrated into the national system—*eg* the Albert I Royal and National Library of Belgium—a pattern repeated in Scandinavia where university library functions are also added. Most attempt to provide international research collections, but note the limitation of the Swiss National Library purely to Helvetica. The divided condition of the Prussian State Library should be appreciated and an article by Felix Reichmann, ' Three hundred years of the Prussian State Library ', in *Library quarterly* 32 (3) July 1962 225-230.

LEGAL DEPOSIT—PROBLEMS AND FUNCTIONS
The *Ordinance de Montpellier* 1537 was the first regulation concerned with legal deposit. Some countries use legal deposit as a censorship device (Japan) others as necessary adjunct to securing copyright protection. Many variations in practice since first adopted in UK in 1610 as a private arrangement between the Stationers Company and Bodley; no penalties for non-compliance until Star Chamber decree 1637. Press Licensing Acts 1662 replace lapsed 1637 decree and require three deposit copies. Copyright Act 1709 increases to nine copies, 1801 Union with Ireland eleven copies, reduced to five 1836; 1911 National Library of Wales added (but under special conditions).

Regarded by publishers as a tax but it is widely practised throughout the world—many countries require more than six copies. Arguments pro and con are summarised in James Olle ' Free books in an affluent society ' *Library world* 64 (750) December 1962, 162-167.

The responsibilities which legal deposit places upon libraries should be appreciated. Its use in ensuring the preservation of records of a nation's culture is undeniable, but it is open to question whether three universities (one of them in a foreign capital) should be subsidised. Should certain regional reference libraries be given the privilege instead? The NCL has been suggested as the recipient of one copy. Should a second copy be available in the BM for international exchange purposes? Should legal deposit be abolished and library purchase grants be raised to level where they can buy everything they need? Assess the value of free publicity of national bibliography entry arising out of deposit. Consider should deposit libraries exercise greater discretion in making claims (cf selective policy of L of C). R C B Partridge examines practice throughout the world in T Landau *Encyclopaedia of librarianship* (Bowes and Bowes) under the heading 'Legal deposit'.

UNIVERSITY LIBRARIES—HISTORY AND FUNCTIONS

Wherever students and scholars gather so do books. Evidence that the Greek academies and Chinese universities had large collections, and that teaching monasteries placed great value on book collections, is examined by H J Vleeschauwer in *Mousaion* (31, 32) 1958 under the title 'Academies and libraries'. This traces the history of the growth of the university idea, and although inaccessible, *Library science abstract 9853* is very full.

Before 1800 only seven universities in British Isles, Oxford (c 1163) Cambridge (1209?) St Andrews (1411) Glasgow (1453) Aberdeen (1494) Edinburgh (1582) and Trinity College Dublin (1591). Foundation of Durham (1832) and London (1836) presages great expansion in next century.

EFFECTS OF UNIVERSITIES ON MEDIEVAL CULTURE

Most immediate effect is trend away from monasteries as places of learning and book production. Monastic method, learned, leisurely, precise, unsuited to the needs of the universities for multiple copies of texts cheaply produced. *Stationarii* employed virtually production line techniques. Their methods are described in F Wormald and C E Wright *The English library before 1700* (Athlone Press 1957).

Impact of the mendicant orders of friars on book trade and higher education is profound. Older orders obliged to try to counteract their influence by establishing colleges at Oxford and

Cambridge. Early growth of these universities stultified by narrow view of learning and religious bigotry accompanying it in Middle Ages.

Really three separate foundations **1** Old Congregation House Library, Thomas Cobham (*d* 1327) **2** Duke Humfrey's Library (1435) dispensed and largely destroyed at Reformation **3** the same re-founded by Thomas Bodley (1600). Thomas James (1573-1629) first librarian of Bodley's Library which attracted many gifts of money and materials in early years. Bodley set character of early selection—rabid anti-catholicism, prejudice against small and English books, penchant for orientalia.

Thomas Hyde, librarian 1665-1701 distinguished orientalist produced printed catalogue 1674. Eighteenth century a quiet period of consolidation. Nineteenth century, Bulkeley Bandinet, librarian 1813-1860, most acquisitive so far. Other librarians E W B Nicholson, a founder of the LA, Madan (1912-1919), Craster (1931-1945) responsible for planning buildings opened 1946 and for *History of the Bodleian Library 1845-1945* (OUP 1952). Collections grouped into printed books, western MSS, orientalia. J N L Myres 'The Bodleian Library' *Library world* 62 (730) April 1961 225-229 and an article in *Times literary supplement* 24th September 1954 describe the present day organisation.

Oxford colleges have libraries in their own right—University College 1249, Balliol 1263 are first; the university has also highly developed departmental libraries and undergraduate facilities.

Origins obscure, first 'hand' references to a library 1381. Catalogue 1424 shows 122 books, 1473—330, 1528—600, 1556 catalogue shows 175 of which 130 are still there. Andrew Perne (*d* 1589) often called second founder of the library for his donations of monastic material. Seventeenth century a time of great expansion. Library trebled in size by donation by George I (1715) of Bishop Moore's 30,000 volumes. Legal deposit applied for 1709, albeit imperfectly. Henry Bradshaw (1868-1886) perhaps greatest librarian, though Francis Jenkinson (1889-1923) did noble work. New buildings 1934. J C T Oates 'The Cambridge University

Library 1400-1600' *Library quarterly* 32 (4) October 1962 270-286 is a useful reading.

PROVINCIAL UNIVERSITIES
Principal feature is growth in numbers from fifteen in 1957 to twenty eight in 1964 with ten Colleges of Advanced Technology added by 1965. Early ones state aided since 1889. First clear statement of importance of the library in a university is University Grants Committee's first report 1921 : —' The character and efficiency of a University may be gauged by its treatment of its central organ, the library . . . an adequate library is not only the basis of all teaching and study; it is the essential condition of research'.

No definitive history has been attempted. There are numerous articles on, and histories of, individual libraries. E G Baxter 'A preliminary historical survey of developments in university libraries in Great Britain, 1919-1950' *Library Association record* 56 (9 & 10) September-October 1954 330-335 and 389-393 covers some of the ground and refers to eighty three other sources. B S Page ' University library developments' *Library Association proceedings, papers and summaries of discussions of the annual conference 1957* 52-58 is helpful background. ' University and research library notes' appearing in *Library Association record* irregularly, provides a commentary on developments. In recent years *Library world* has featured many libraries. For example, ' University College library' in *Library world* 65 (765) March 1964 296-298.

It is to the new universities that we must look for innovation and a break from traditional attitudes. New universities are fortunate when they are able to rely upon established libraries in their formative years, for example Manchester with Rylands, Chethams and the City Library, and the latest Universities with the NLL. O S Tomlinson examines the relationships between public libraries and universities in his paper *Public libraries and higher education* given to the 1964 public libraries conference at Rothesay.

UNITED STATES
Most striking is the slow beginning—Harvard (established 1636) had only 50,000 volumes in 1850—considering the massive size of the present major libraries—Harvard six and a half million,

Yale four and a half million volumes and nearly twenty others with more than one million volumes compared with only three British with more than one million volumes. Strong growth began in the late nineteenth century. Later start does not mean older background material is missing—outstanding rare book collections in many places. Many collections highly departmentalised or organised on a subject divisional basis. History and functions of the American university library dealt with by L R Wilson and M F Tauber *The University library* (Columbia University Press). K W Humphreys indicates highlights in his article 'University libraries' in *Encyclopedia of librarianship* (Bowes and Bowes). A subjective view of one library is given by S Daniels 'The way of an American university: impressions of an exchange librarian' *Library Association record* 60 (1) January 1958 4-7. A broader picture is painted by Catherine Bishop 'University libraries of the United States' *New Zealand libraries* 27 (10) November 1964 269-274.

OTHER COUNTRIES

The special state/public/university library structure as applied in Germany should be appreciated, together with their institute libraries set apart from the main library and independent of it. Structure throughout Europe is discussed in an issue of *Library trends* entitled 'European university libraries'.

F J E Hirst 'University libraries in Eire' *Library world* 65 (766) April 1964 331-335 and liberal coverage in K C Harrison *Scandinavian libraries* (Deutsch 1961) also helps. Growth in the Commonwealth since 1945 should also be noted. Jean Bleton 'New universities in France' UNESCO *Bulletin* 13 (5-6) May-June 1959 115-119 is also interesting.

FUNCTIONS OF THE UNIVERSITY LIBRARY

The concept of the library as the 'soul' of the university, the sun around which all research and teaching revolves, is widely acknowledged. Lip service to such sentiments fit strangely with the severe cuts of University Grants Committee estimates, such as those in 1963, which affected libraries adversely, as they did all university departments. At the same time as the cuts were imposed, exhortations to increase student enrolments were heard increasingly from government. The vaunted 'Robbins report ' *Higher education* (HMSO *cmnd* 2154) virtually ignores library matters. James Thompson hits hard at its woolly ' double think ' in ' University libraries and higher education ' *Library Association record* 66 (11) November 1964 466-471. This article does, however, criticise the lack of direction apparent in some university thinking.

TECHNICAL AND TRAINING COLLEGES

Properly organised libraries are of recent origin. Some technical colleges and their libraries founded on mechanics institute origins. As recently as 1954 only 160 out of 555 technical colleges had more than 300 books in their libraries and only fifty two had chartered librarians. Conditions in the mid 1950's are summarised in the *Library Association record* 58 (3) March 1956 100-102 in an article called ' Colleges of technology and further education '. Progress since then rapid, position much improved, see *Libraries in colleges of technology, commerce and art* 1958-9 (London and Home Counties regional advisory council for technological education). The creation of colleges of advanced technology (CAT's) indicated new points of departure for library development in colleges as shown in E G Baxter ' Technical college libraries and the future of higher education ' *Library Association record* 65 (2) February 1963 60-66. F Earnshaw in a letter to the *Library Association record* in May 1963 (page 205) pointed out how far British college libraries had still to go to compare with the largest American and European institutions and he supported his contention with facts and figures.

The functions of technical college libraries and their growing similarity with those of universities are indicated by such articles as A C Bubb ' Research and the technical college library ' *Librarian* 50 (2) February 1961 21-23 and F Earnshaw ' Service to technology ' *Librarian* 50 (1) January 1960 1-6.

Training college libraries are also of recent origin. Introduction of three year courses and shift of emphasis to study in depth indicates need for better library services. A memorandum by the LA and Association of Teachers in Colleges and Departments of Education, *Library Association record* 63 (12) December 1961 419-422, should be studied for its comments on functions of the library. Two papers at the LA conference 1961 outline the goals of the training college library C Bibby and A E Sanderson

Training college libraries: developments and prospects, published in the *Proceedings of the annual conference 1961* (LA 1961). Major unresolved issue is the unwillingness of the professional educator to acknowledge librarians rather than teachers as best staff for a training college library.

THE FUTURE OF TECHNICAL AND TRAINING COLLEGE LIBRARIES
The implications of the Robbins Report and the impact of CNAA need to be studied. Increasing student populations produce the need to encourage more 'self organisation' of study using the library. The improved standards of university libraries means that university trained staffs in colleges expect better library facilities for their own research. Little attention has been paid to the potent influence which a good library can exert in attracting high quality staff and research students to an institution.

Definitive treatment of problems in non-university higher education libraries is given by the recent (February 1965) publication of D L Smith and E G Baxter *College library administration in colleges of technology, art, commerce and further education* (OUP 1965) which does not, however, shed any light on the history of these institutions.

CHAPTER TWO: GOVERNMENT FINANCE AND ORGANISATION

MAINLY under the control of the Ministry of Education, though many national library staffs do not enjoy status and privileges equal to other civil servants. Examination of the government and organisation of several libraries illustrates certain differences in approach.

The British Museum: Administered by a director and principal librarian with a principal keeper (printed books) four keepers (two printed books and one each manuscripts and orientalia) and a secretary. Total staff about 270 appointed by Civil Service Commission, except for director (a Crown appointment always from within the Museum staff).

Government is carried out under the terms of the British Museum Act 1963 which has reduced the size of the governing body by withdrawing the rights of certain state and clerical officers and the families of benefactors to seats. Under its terms the Museum is more free to participate in the national system of libraries than hitherto, being empowered to loan, sell or otherwise dispose of unwanted materials. Authority granted to purchase land to build new library. The BM still comes directly under Treasury control and seeks its funds annually therefrom—a suggestion that they be given a quinquennial grant not taken up.

National Library of Wales: Staff consists of librarian, deputy, three department heads and assistants. Although not civil servants, salaries are linked to the civil service provincial grades with a private superannuation scheme. Total staff about seventy five.

Government through a court of governors consisting of a president, vice president, treasurer, appointees from the Privy Council, university and colleges, local authorities, lords lieutenant and sheriffs, the thirty six Welsh MP's, representatives of substantial benefactors and twenty one co-opted members. The executive council of thirty three members meets five times a year as does the finance committee.

Most benefactions and endowments are mortgaged for years ahead to complete buildings—Treasury have made little contribution to building funds but supply virtually all running expenses, with some assistance from the Friends of the National Library of Wales and the Friends of the National Libraries. Purchase funds represent about eight percent of total expenditure (plus benefit of legal deposit).

National Library of Scotland: Two departments, printed books and manuscripts. Librarian assisted by two keepers and about seventy other staff.

Government through a board of trustees under terms of the National Library of Scotland Act 1925. Composition of the board includes representatives of faculty of advocates, the universities, local authorities, trustees appointed by the Crown and several ex officio members. Finance is almost entirely provided by Treasury grant with about £5,000 coming from endowments.

Library of Congress: Organisation is indicated in chapter one. Staff totals more than 2,500, appointed directly by the librarian; they are outside the American civil service. Government is unique. Librarian is responsible directly to Congress, though appointed by the President with Senate approval. Relations with Congress are regulated through a joint congressional committee, though the librarian has very wide discretionary powers.

Finance is raised through appropriations committees of both Houses and not subject to revision by Bureau of Budget. Funds are applied at the discretion of the librarian. Endowments provide some income and include amounts to pay stipends to consultants without administrative responsibility, and for supplementation of official salaries of subject specialists.

The library is organised in divisions by subject and function.

In *National libraries: their problems and prospects* (UNESCO 1960) F C Francis discusses (*pp* 21-26) the organisation of national libraries and maintains that the divisional plan, and indeed the L of C in general, most nearly approaches the ideal in a national library. He refers to difficulty of swift, informed service in the large general library. He claims that divisional plan leads to greater satisfaction through intensive service for both staff and readers.

Despite greater demands on buildings and staff, divisional plan is inevitable for really efficient service in large libraries. Significant that two libraries regarded as being in the forefront, the L of C and the Lenin Library, are both so organised and now the BM is interested in adopting such a plan. The National Diet Library Tokyo shows a different type of specialisation. All government department libraries are administered by the Diet Library as branch libraries. The difficulty caused by the present British plan of division—into printed book, manuscripts, state papers etc, is that it cuts across subjects.

FINANCE OF NATIONAL LIBRARIES

In almost every case the majority of finance comes from government grant. Purchase funds average twenty percent of total expenditure in a sample of twenty national libraries for the year 1962 with variations from seven percent to fifty percent. The BM proportion is about ten percent, L of C eight percent (including books for the blind special fund), BN nine percent, and at the other extreme Australian National Library thirty three percent, Korean thirty percent, Laotian fifty percent. It seems that older, more developed collections need less for purchasing, but that large stocks require very high staff inputs.

Unspent appropriations at the end of the year must usually be returned to the Treasury. Libraries are thus unable to build up funds for expensive purchases unless special provision is made —as in BM and BN. Endowment funds are not a significant source of revenue in most libraries. National Library of Scotland derives about three percent of funds in this way, L of C six percent. Activities of organisations of friends are invaluable, especially when money is needed for expensive purchases. Gifts, appeals and bequests are important especially for building purposes. National Libraries of Scotland and Wales largely so built. BM owes its origin to a state lottery!

UNIVERSITY LIBRARIES—GOVERNMENT

All British universities have a library committee formed from the Senate or similar body. In the United States pattern varies; sometimes the librarian is responsible directly to a president, or to a library committee—of trustees or of the Senate or Academic

24

Council. Various patterns are fully described in Wilson and Tauber *The University library* (Columbia University Press). How different are British and European patterns of government is shown by the points stressed in an article by an Austrian librarian, Franz Kroller, ' On the administration of English university libraries' *Biblos* 11 (4) 1962 211-221. The article is in German but a long abstract in *Library science abstracts* No. 12873 is available. In Austrian university libraries, for example, which are constitutionally separate from the university, the librarian is responsible to the Ministry of Education directly, with the minimum of official contact with faculty members.

FINANCE OF UNIVERSITY LIBRARIES
Allocated by the University Grants Committee in quinquennial cycles from money made available by the Treasury. Estimates are prepared by each university in a form prescribed by the UGC who then make a visitation to examine the university's case and confirm, amend or refer back the estimate for further consideration. A full history and description of the mode of working of the UGC is given in *University development 1957-1962 (cmnd 2267 HMSO 1964).*

Advantages claimed for this system are that they oblige the university to think deeply about policy and that, once an appropriation is granted, there is some security from chance economic illwinds which is not available to national and college libraries which operate on annual budgeting. If, however, the quinquennial allocations are made against the background of a particularly unfavourable economic climate, estimates, especially for capital works, can suffer terribly.

Once the university library budget is settled steps can be taken to allocate it. The practice of dividing the purchase fund into a general purpose fund and a periodical account and then dividing it amongst departments, while still widely used, has given way in some universities to a situation in which all purchase funds are held centrally and disbursed at the discretion of the librarian. This has come about because the larger funds available in recent years have allowed a broader, more flexible, attitude to be adopted so that every department can expect to receive sufficient for its basic needs at least.

The case for and against dividing the purchase funds into a number of departmental funds is as follows. *Advantages*: **1** Allows closer contact between librarian and ensures the best use of specialist advice **2** Ensures that unusually voracious departments do not obtain an undue share of funds by making them stay within the bounds of a pre-arranged budget **3** Librarian can oversee trends in departments seeing clearly where the need for more funds lies for the purposes of justifying future estimates **4** Proportion of funds retained centrally can be used as a balancing item to correct any bias which might creep into a fund used by a department. It can also be used to provide supporting bibliographical materials and to provide a fund for especially expensive purchases.

Disadvantages: **1** Limits the abilities of progressive departments to build up their stocks, while less good departments spend their allocation non-purposively simply to 'get their share' **2** Inevitable but expensive purchases can absorb a large part of the departmental fund to the detriment of a purchasing programme **3** Can result in wholesale duplication and overlap unless carefully watched.

Four percent of total university expenditure has been put forward as the minimum necessary to support a proper library programme. A survey in *Liaison* July 1964 38 revealed that in 1961/62 library budgets in British universities varied from 1·9 percent to 8·6 percent of total university expenditure. According to W J Scott 'Value for money in university libraries' *Library world* 65 (768) June 1964 387-389 about half the total university library appropriation goes on staff salaries. The average amount per student available for book purchases in 1961/62 was £10 per student, though individual universities varied from £6 to £14 5s. The AUT survey makes reference to the most important point that libraries do enjoy considerable economies of scale. Therefore direct inter-university comparisons can be misleading.

Endowment funds, except in Oxford, Cambridge, Hull and Liverpool, make little contribution to university funds. Only in these four institutions do they amount to more than four percent of total expenditure, and Cambridge's 7.3 percent for 1962/63 is the highest for a British university. A number of university libraries do now have associations of Friends. Special appeals for funds for general university purposes have been made, especially by new universities, *eg* East Anglia, Lancaster and York, and some of the funds are occasionally used for library purposes. Special grants from charitable trusts and government research bodies can often benefit libraries. The various financial sources are examined in a symposium ' Extra-university sources of finance' *College and research libraries* 23 (6) November 1962 509-521.

ORGANISATION AND ADMINISTRATION OF UNIVERSITY LIBRARIES

Most difficult organisational problem is what decentralisation there should be in university library structure. Desirability of departmental libraries is discussed in chapter six.

British and American university libraries are often praised for their liberal loans policies and high degree of open access to the shelves. German university libraries are also liberal in loans policy but have almost totally closed access, though the institute libraries are often open access for reference only. Opening hours gradually extending in Britain. Eighty hours a week is now quite common, while in America a hundred hours a week opening can be found. Provision of quiet study rooms, with or without direct reader service and open for longer hours than the library is a sensible facility which is increasingly practised. A postal loans service during vacations is a development viewed favourably by some universities.

TECHNICAL SERVICES IN UNIVERSITY LIBRARIES

Library binderies are now common. In America they are often provided for economy, but in Britain accessibility is the principal reason, since commercial binderies are more economic, unit for unit, in Britain.

Increasing mechanisation of cataloguing and acquisitions processes through computers is being used in some places. Edward Heilinger 'Application of advanced data processing techniques to university library procedures' *Special libraries* 53 (8) October 1962 472-473, Phillip M Mase 'The prospects for mechanisation' *College and research libraries* 25 (2) March 1964 115-119 and the three articles on data processing at Florida Atlantic University (where Heilinger is librarian) *College and research libraries* 25 (3) May 1964 181-199, indicate scope for such developments. Mechanisation has not gone very far in Britain yet, though xerox, flexowriters and electronic stencil cutters are common enough. Perhaps reason why full potentialities of micro-recording and data processing not yet realised is because of past emphasis upon academic learning rather than technical skill as the hallmark of senior university librarians. It is probably for the same reason that few of our university librarians speak or write authoritatively upon classification theories or techniques. Practice varies from complete absence of classification, through use of home made schemes, to examples of the use of each of the major general schemes. J Thompson questions the value of close classification in university libraries in an article ' Classification in the new university libraries ' *Library Association record* 65 (9) September 1963 327-329.

Many academic libraries have rejected use of general schemes in favour of home made schemes which more clearly express relationships with organisation of teaching in their university (*cf* Leeds, University College London, York). Incentive to use standard cataloguing practices based on a published code and a general classification scheme is not so pronounced in Britain as in America, where the use of L of C catalogue cards can lead to considerable economies. The BNB card service in Britain is of very limited value, given the international nature of book selection policies.

COLLEGE LIBRARIES

The chapter in *Five years of work in librarianship 1956-1960* (LA 1963) on libraries in colleges of technology and further education should be studied. Library staff status not completely settled in Britain and department head status not common. Access to department heads' meetings more common but not sufficient alternative to full acceptance. Some college libraries still regarded as extension of the college office and staffed by typists and clerks.

Library committees in colleges, where they exist at all, usually consist of staff below department head status. They therefore lack a strong voice in external policy formation, but through intimate acquaintance with the library's teaching function can have good effects on its internal policy concerning library use. Librarian usually reports direct to the principal or vice principal, sometimes to a department head.

Organisation varies. In some counties, college libraries are centrally administered either directly through the education department or at one remove through the county library (*eg* Durham and Northants). In other counties each college library is administered as a separate entity. Similar situation in county boroughs, though they are usually independently administered since the constitutional position of public libraries in relation to the education authority is different. In county boroughs public libraries are not usually subordinated to the education authority. A number of interesting joint schemes have been developed (West Bromwich, Belfast).

FINANCE OF COLLEGE LIBRARIES, ADMINISTRATION AND BUILDINGS

Standards for library service in colleges of technology and further education were worked out in 1959 by the Library Association and revised in 1964. They incorporate recommended standards for initial stock, book funds, building and accommodation requirements etc. Earlier edition very conservative; 1964 edition hardly visionary and likely to fall short of expansionary phase just beginning. It is possible that reference to such standards might inhibit rather than promote progress.

Financial provision for college libraries usually one percent to two percent of total college expenditure. It may be argued that narrower base of technical college operations implies that comparison with university expenditure standards is not appropriate. But development of liberal studies programmes, CNAA degree courses and possibility of a number of colleges reaching university status, indicates that such arguments may be misconceived. Indeed, following out the ' economy of scale ' arguments of the AUT survey *The University library* (AUT 1964), there is reason to argue that expenditure proportions should be at least the same as those recommended for universities.

Building standards incorporated in Ministry of Education Circular 322 have proved highly inadequate in practice. The Ministry's *Building bulletin No. 5* improved on the figure given in Circular 322 of thirty two square feet per reader, but still inadequate. All official and unofficial statements seem to have severely underestimated the growth rate of higher education. Many libraries built into new colleges three or four years ago are already proving inadequate. Principal shortcomings are too modest provision of storage space and staff work space and, especially, bad siting. Libraries should be adjacent to the main thoroughfares but, too often, are placed high in a tower block.

TECHNICAL SERVICES IN COLLEGE LIBRARIES

Small staffs make streamlining imperative. Classification is usually close, with UDC the most favoured scheme. Cataloguing practice varies but larger colleges especially have found use of BNB cards not economic due to their large requirements for foreign literature. The problem is discussed by G Hill ' The use of BNB cards at Manchester College of Science and Technology' *Librarian* 46 (10) 1957 192-195.

TRAINING COLLEGES

Development on sound lines. Of more recent origin than the technical colleges, but, due probably to the greater degree of uniformity in the courses offered, progress has been more even throughout the country. No outstanding libraries as yet. Swift expansion of college populations coupled with three year courses and development of more intensive study, teaching and research has placed a great strain on library services. The university institutes of education (established in 1947) have helped considerably. Educational developments, following the Robbins Report recommendations for training colleges, will need to be balanced carefully against library developments.

Organisation and routine in training college libraries is dealt with by W H Shercliffe *Education libraries bulletin* 19 (Spring) 1964 1-24. Educationists are by no means yet convinced that the best pattern of library provision is based upon professional librarianship. A memorandum from the School Library Association *Memorandum on the impact of the three year course on the function of the training college library* (1960) by T H Simms, advocates staffing libraries with trained teachers, and a number of them are so staffed.

' Training college libraries: recommendations on their development' *Library Association record* 63 (12) December 1961 419-422 discusses the function of these libraries and proposes standards for their premises and equipment. Accommodation is recommended as forty square feet for twenty five percent of college population plus storage and staff rooms. N Roberts ' Classification in training college libraries' *Education libraries bulletin* 19 (Spring) 1964 25-29 examines practice in existing libraries.

An excellent section of commentary and references is given in *Five years of work in librarianship 1956-1960* (LA 1963) in a chapter headed ' Education libraries '.

CHAPTER THREE: PLANNING EQUIPMENT AND FITTINGS

PROBLEM for large libraries is conflicting requirements of large, easily expandable storage areas and swift reader service. In view of Fremont Rider's assertion that American college and university libraries tend to double their size every fifteen years (made first in *About books* 11 (1) 1940 1-11), the great need in planning new buildings is to provide sufficient storage areas and room for expansion. H W Axford ' Rider revisited' *College and research libraries* 23 (4) July 1962 345-347 examines the validity of Rider's claim in the light of growth between 1946 and 1960. Conclusions are that the average growth rate over the period was seventy eight percent but some greatly exceeded 100 percent (one achieved 190 percent). General conclusion was, however, that the larger the library becomes the slower its growth rate—Yale twenty four percent, Harvard forty four percent, Illinois sixty four percent, Columbia sixty eight percent. Some problems of swift growth in terms of building problems are given by Ralph E McCoy ' The ordeal of a university library' *Library journal* 85 (9) May 1st 1960 1729-1734. He presents problems accruing to a library 170,000 volumes strong in 1955, then 350,000 volumes in 1959 with a probable one million in 1970. Modular planning has been adopted by McCoy's library (Southern Illinois University) and the library is settled at the heart of the campus. The modular concept is fully explained in UNESCO *Bulletin* 17 (6) November-December 1963 346-350.

SITE SELECTION

Keyes D Metcalf ' Selection of library sites' *College and research libraries* 22 (3) May 1961 183-192 argues against central campus location as an ideal. He says **1** Temptation to build an unfunctional monument is irresistible to an architect if library is the central building **2** Need for access for all sides increases the need for lobby and circulation space and increases supervision problems **3** Likely to be difficult to provide for expansion.

As for almost everything the chapter on site selection in Wilson and Tauber, *The University library,* is excellent. R E Ellsworth *Planning the college and university library building: a book for campus planners and architects* (Colorado, The Pruett Press) is also very good. This latter author ' Consultants for college and university library building planning ' *College and research libraries* 21(4) July 1960 263-268 includes a summary of accommodation requirements which need to be programmed in planning a new building. This article is vital reading. The programme can be usefully compared with A Thompson ' The systematic description of library buildings' *Library Association record* 64 (12) December 1962 450-452. Although designed for the description of completed buildings it serves as a guide to the services to be incorporated into a new building and is, therefore, a useful check list for the planning stage.

In the same issue of *College and research libraries* (July 1960) Miss E Green ' Background activities in the planning of a new library', pages 269-274, discusses the librarian's contribution to the establishment of new buildings and, by exemplifying the Barnard College Library, describes the steps needed to turn a programme such as Ellsworth's into terms of sizes and costs. Ralph R Shaw *State of the library art* volume three, parts one to three, ' Buildings, shelving and storage warehouses' is important. H R Galvin and K A Devereaux's *Planning a library building* (ALA 1955) analyses the roles of the librarian and the architect at every stage of planning and building.

ALTERNATIVES TO A NEW LIBRARY BUILDING

Not everyone is fortunate enough to be able to plan completely new buildings. For many, adaptation and contrivance of small existing buildings to fit present and future needs is the chief preoccupation. Aside from the problems of providing for the needs of a larger library staff, with concomitant increases in space for technical service operations, main problems are more storage space and more reader space—two objectives which, on the surface, are in direct conflict if both are to be provided within the confines of an existing building. The heading to this section is the title of an article by Keyes D Metcalf *College and research libraries* 22 (5) September 1961 345-354. A valid point made by Metcalf is that a study of the alternatives to new building is an essential preliminary to any claim for new construction. If the claim is rejected, a quick follow-up with less expensive alternatives has a good chance of success. Such studies are especially apposite to small college libraries confined to rooms in larger blocks rather than located on individual sites.

ALTERNATIVES SUMMARISED

Reading areas: Radical re-thinking of existing layouts to make more efficient use of space by:

1 Refurnishing, which will often create more reader space through use of more utilitarian, less ornate furniture.

2 Use of lobbies, corridors and aisles in old buildings. Lobbies and corridors can become exhibition areas, thus releasing exhibition rooms for reader space, or become catalogue halls or enquiry and service counter areas. Non public corridors can be shelved if, thereby, reader space can be provided in storage areas.

3 Mezzanines can often be introduced into high ceilinged rooms.

4 In small colleges library rooms may be exchanged with other, larger rooms *eg* assembly halls, lecture theatres, large classrooms, even machine rooms.

5 Storage accommodation may be moved elsewhere—this can, however, reduce the effectiveness of reader service.

6 Departmental libraries and subject divisions being established away from the main library in less confined surroundings. (Faculties likely to benefit will aid fight for necessary funds far more readily than for a central library building.)

Storage areas

1 Compact storage introduced—rolling stacks—double banking —higher shelves—segregation of books by size to economise on space (but these reduce the efficiency of stores).

2 Removal of older stock to out of town stores.

3 Introduction of ' crash ' micro-filming projects.

4 Disposal of some older stock coupled with increased reliance upon co-operation or co-operative stores.

5 Reducing intake by more stringent selection (are our present selection methods fully efficient?)

6 Reduction of bulk of stored materials by binding, for example, periodicals, patents.

Staff and technical services space: Likely to be most difficult since this is traditionally the meanest original provision.

1 Re-location of technical services elsewhere.

2 Introduction of mechanisation to reduce labour input into technical services—same staff and space but aim is more productivity.

3 Careful rearrangement of work areas using methods of industrial management consultancy.

4 Examination of existing office accommodation with a view to dividing offices to house extra staff.

The foregoing assumes the impossibility of alternatives such as the addition of annexes or additional storeys. Where decentralisation, co-operative stores, re-location of service areas is practised, the uses of closed circuit television, telex, telex/xerox and photocopying should not be overlooked as means of reducing staff/reader inconvenience.

Expensive nature of alternatives will sometimes lead to the conclusion that new buildings are necessary. This in turn will lead to an examination of the ideal in new building.

NEW NATIONAL LIBRARY BUILDING

Only one real ideal is a site and building capable of great expansion and easy re-planning of interior layouts. Island site and modular are principles therefore called for.

The principal need in a national library is for storage and technical service accommodation rather than for very large reading areas, although this does depend on the location. If the library is in the centre of a large population area—near a university perhaps—then the need for reading areas can be greater than in a relatively small population centre (*eg* Aberystwyth or Canberra). Special provision for long term research needs will be required and possibly even rentable private offices.

Siting is best in a large centre of population such as the capital city but this can limit growth, *eg* the British Museum's recent difficulties in obtaining land for extension, compared with the virtually limitless growth potential for the NLL at rural Boston Spa. A note on the requirements of national library buildings is given in UNESCO *Bulletin* 18 (4) July-August 1964 157. This is a summary of a paper given at the Asian regional seminar. The full paper included a twenty four point summary of planning principles and procedures.

Provision in national libraries will often need to include accommodation for a national bibliographic centre and for other 'service' organisations for a country's library system. Also perhaps a school of librarianship.

Scale of accommodation: This depends on many things, *eg* is it the policy of the institution to restrict borrowing rights? National libraries usually do restrict but in any case their planning problems have so far proved virtually insoluble. In academic libraries scale also depends on the teaching policy, *eg* is it based upon lectures and small reading lists or upon project based courses involving a high degree of self help and guidance by tutorials? In terms of seating accommodation the difference between the two systems' needs might be ten percent of student population for the former to 50 percent for the latter system. The AUT survey recommends seating accommodation in library of thirty three percent of total number of student population. Keyes D Metcalf 'Seating accommodation' *College and research libraries* 23 (5) September 1963 375-382 should be studied. The special issue of UNESCO *Bulletin* 17 (6) December 1963 has articles on planning a project, climatic factors, lighting, storage and a discussion of the relative merits of fixed function and modular construction. M Rojnic 'Various types of reading rooms in university libraries' *Libri* 14 (1) 1964 76-85, 'University library buildings' *Libri* 9 (1) 1959 99-30, J F E Hirst 'The new library, Trinity College Dublin' *An Leabharlann* 18 (1) March 1960 15, are all articles worth reading. For inspiration on modes of equipping and laying out libraries see W Mevissen *Buchereibau* (Essen Heyer).

Other points to note: Demand in academic libraries is for study areas open late—not necessarily with full library service. Need is for heated space, lit and silent (bearing in mind that living accommodation is frequently poor). Need also for smoking rooms, rooms for use of typewriters and business machines. Need for seminar rooms where special collections can be brought together quickly for specific short term needs of a tutor. When a campus is widespread or where a library attracts visitors from other places, car parks are needed.

For a detailed summary of available descriptions of new buildings see ' Non public library buildings in the UK: a select bibliography 1950-1960 ' *Library Association record* 63 (2) February 1961 48-49.

CHAPTER FOUR: STAFF

LACK of any serious literature from British sources on staffing matters points to undervaluation of human resources in libraries. Available literature seeks to explain the functions and responsibilities of various grades of staff without analysing problems. American writing much concerned with status issues.

Adequate appreciation of staffing issues should include awareness of broader problems of personnel administration outside librarianship—human relations, communications, welfare, management development. This awareness should be synthesised to relate it to problems within librarianship. Librarian/administrators should read such periodicals as *Manager, Business* and *Public administration*. Books to be read with profit are R F Tredgold *Human relations in modern industry* (Duckworth), P Garforth *Management development* (Institute of Personnel Management), T M Ling *Mental health and human relations in industry* (H K Lewis) and W V Merrihue *Managing by communication* (McGraw-Hill).

Librarians need to overcome aversion to personnel administration as a scientific study and to realise that librarianship can benefit from experience in other fields. The multiplicity of writings on the problems of recruiting and employing graduates in industry are directly relevant. Professional librarianship has too often failed to recruit graduates of adequate capability. Greater awareness of the methods, objectives and prospects of graduates in industry, government and the academic sphere would help towards recognition of the present shortcomings of graduate careers offered in academic and national libraries.

STAFFING PROBLEMS

1 *Interactions of various grades*: Problem aggravated by many staff divisions—graduate, non-graduate, professional, clerical-manual, skilled, manual, unskilled. Another division is arising between good honours and ordinary graduates. With these divisions a community of interest is difficult to create.

British national and university libraries do not have a good record in providing facilities for staff to train for promotion, especially in order to read for degrees or pursue research for higher degrees. They have been the leaders in Britain of a programme of rationalisation of grades and duties but have failed signally to provide the essential corollary to it—that facilities are available to anyone to obtain qualifications to progress through the grades.

To a certain extent in the past these libraries were able to attract partly or fully qualified non-graduate staff from, typically, public libraries. They could usually offer better working conditions and slightly higher commencing salaries but the signs are that pay, conditions and prospects are now improving in other areas so as to make the limited prospects in national and academic libraries less attractive to good non-graduate personnel.

Suggested standards of qualification and status for British university library staffs are given in *The University library* (Association of University Teachers 1964). American problems and attitudes are examined by R H Serbert in ' Status and responsibilities of academic librarians' *College and research libraries* 22 (4) July 1961 253-258.

2 *Subject specialisation*: Some national and most university libraries practise a degree of subject division with specialist staff, though a serious problem is the lack of specialists in science, orientalia, maps, manuscripts and rare book librarianship. Specialists run the risk of being kept aside from the main promotion stream through lack of opportunity to prove general administrative ability. Their main compensations are the bargaining power of scarcity and the satisfaction to be derived from their ability to give service in depth in a manner not open to their generalist colleagues. They are better able to fulfil themselves by research and to benefit from closer relations with the users of their collections.

As a comment on specialisation it is interesting to note that many senior non-graduates in academic libraries compensate for lack of a degree by studying to attain unassailable authority in various librarianship techniques (*eg* reprography or classification).

3 *Status and salaries*: Equation of higher grades in national libraries with the salaries of academic library personnel with similar experience is by no means a common occurrence in many countries. Principal problem seems to be integration with civil service gradings at too low a level, or sometimes absence of any equation with

existing schemes. Concrete instances of difficulties reported in *Library trends* 4 (1) 1955 81-88.

American preoccupation with status of academic librarians indicates lack of equation with faculty staff at a satisfactory level. While a similar feeling exists in lesser colleges in Britain, the younger elements in universities must find such readings rather strange. High academic status and salary, and membership of the appropriate governing and administrative organs, are now widespread in Britain. Less common is satisfactory equation with teaching staffs for subordinate library staff. The joint LA/AUT recommendations on salaries of graduate library staffs in universities, reported in *Library Association record* 65 (3) March 1963 108, recommends as basic qualification a good honours degree plus a research degree or professional qualification—the same as for teaching staff appointments.

The status of American academic librarians is examined by R B Downs in ' The Status of American college and university librarians ' ACRL *Monograph* (22) 1958. That the preoccupation with low status is not purely an American phenomenon is demonstrated by an anonymous article 'A Profile of the university libraries in one country ' UNESCO *Bulletin* 17 (3) May-June 1963 169-174.

The major unresolved problem of academic library staffing in the UK is that of standards in technical and training colleges. Some are beginning to obtain standards, both for numbers and grading of staff, comparable with universities but most are far from doing so. Many are still graded on a par with senior administrative staff in their colleges. Many are worked single-handed and, incredibly, a few still have no librarian at all.

The need to obtain adequate salaries for college librarians is, at best, an indication of ends justifying means, at worst it is an admission that librarianship is not, of itself, at a level high enough to merit academic status.

4 *Closed nature of national library appointments*: The *Library trends* article cited above indicates that retention of staff in national libraries is an international problem. In the UK career prospects are reasonable but hardly exciting. The pension arrangements and the nature of the work itself, however, tend to encourage staff to spend their whole careers in one institution. This has good and bad effects. It is good in that continuity of experience is assured, bad in that there is a lack of the cross fertilisation of ideas

which results from staff interchange between various types and sizes of library. The great success of some of the outside appointments to the top posts in the L of C and the success of L of C trained staff in universities in America suggests that there are indeed benefits in exchange.

TECHNICAL COLLEGES

Recommendations on the staffing of technical college libraries *Library Association record* 62 (1) January 1960 21-22 envisaged a staffing standard of only about one third of that considered minimally adequate for a university library; also anticipated that staff functions would also include some teaching. Only about one half of librarians are paid Burnham scale salaries, the rest are on AP & T scales (the same as higher administrative staff of the colleges), a clear indication of the status accorded to them.

TRAINING COLLEGES

The Library Association has also evolved a series of recommended standards for minimum establishment scales for libraries in an article ' Libraries in training colleges ' *Library Association record* 66 (4) April 1964 174-176. One professional staff member to every 250-300 students is the standard recommended.

CHAPTER FIVE: STOCK

THE late Lord Leverhulme used to say that half the money he spent on advertising was wasted, but the trouble was he did not know which half. Modern research libraries faced with an increasing flow of new publications to select from know the feeling. A proportion of their current selections will be little used, even unused, but it is not easy to decide which they will be. Certainly a proportion of the efforts which the large research library puts into acquiring material from all over the world comes to nothing. Could scientific methods be used to decide in advance material which will be of significance? Probably not (as yet) but there are many studies which aspire to recognise the material which can safely be weeded from existing stocks.

Librarians collect widely and irrationally, sometimes out of fear that they might be accused of Bodley's famous mistakes, and perhaps also because they themselves have experienced the deficiencies of their predecessors. They resort to partial solutions of their worst problems in book selection by overstressing the role of inter library co-operation, or subject specialisation schemes, or storage libraries, or micro recording.

The central problem of book selection for the research library is pinpointed by J H P Pafford in his most important article, ' Book selection in the university library' UNESCO *Bulletin* 17 (1) January-February 1963 12-16. Major reference works, important evaluatively reviewed books by acknowledged authorities, and well tried undergraduate texts virtually select themselves. It is the large mass of secondary material and items from new, unknown, sources which pose the problem. This is where lies the dross of the next generation's libraries, inextricably mixed with an indeterminate quantity of its gold.

Pafford also draws attention to the relationship between acquisition and withdrawal policy. Most of the scientifically planned investigations into problems of book selection concern periodicals. Articles such as L Miles Raisig ' Mathematical evaluation of the scientific serial ' *Science* 13 (341) May 13th 1960 1417-1419 and E P Tober ' Determining optimal back number inventories ' *American documentation* 10 (3) July 1959 224-227 illustrate the problems and point to solutions. Dr D J Urquhart's and R M Bunn's researches into the ' half life ' of periodicals has become a standard concept. 'A national loan policy for scientific serials ' *Journal of documentation* 15 (1) March 1959 21-37 is the original reference and this concept has been well supported by other, more limited, studies by various special libraries.

NATIONAL LIBRARIES

An increasing proportion of national library accessions arise out of exchange agreements. UNESCO has been active in promoting international exchanges. Their *Handbook on the international exchange of publications* is supported by regular notes in UNESCO *Bulletin*. Obviously where a library has significant material to offer and can obtain useful items in exchange, much benefit accrues, especially in offsetting the financial stringency usually imposed upon national libraries. Large amount of staff time involved in exchange schemes often disproportionate to the benefits gained but where it is the only way to obtain required material difficulties must be tolerated. Countries with currency exchange difficulties frequently use this method of acquisition. Certain countries use copies obtained under legal deposit as exchange material.

Legal deposit is an important acquisition source, though a number of national libraries do not have deposit privilege. Privilege brings problems—material received causes storage difficulties. Often, withdrawal of unwanted items is not allowed by deposit terms. Because deposited items must be preserved, heavily used materials must be duplicated. Where only one copy is required to be deposited in one library, risk of total destruction is great.

Significance as means of ensuring preservation for posterity has declined somewhat as more libraries take part in co-operative acquisition and retention programmes. More significant for the good of a national library system is the increased emphasis in national libraries upon acquisition of foreign material. It was at Library of Congress that first propositions of Farmington Plan emerged. The sources from which significant materials can be obtained have multiplied and diversified in recent years. The countries with old established book trades show a great increase in number of books published and number of publishers. In newer countries amount and significance of materials has increased.

Studies by Farmington Plan administration in recent years reveal unexpectedly rich materials in, for example, Middle East and South East Asia. National libraries hold primary responsibility for monitoring flow of foreign literature and facilitating its acquisition.

It is because the means of acquisition are often difficult, through lack of reliable book trade, or financial controls, or even political uncertainties, which make direct dealings with book trade sources impossible, that national libraries must take lead in acquiring foreign material. As illustration, Arab materials can only be acquired by Israeli National Library indirectly; they are bought in London and Paris.

Even so if no political or financial restrictions are imposed on the free passage of literature, and UNESCO has worked hard to break down barriers, national libraries must still accept prime responsibility. Libraries often lack essential bibliographic records or have not resources of staff to maintain relationships with foreign book trade sources. They often miss vital material, therefore, and when later they feel need of it the national library will be looked to.

ACADEMIC LIBRARIES

Main problem is to strike balance between undergraduate and research needs. Further problem is balance of funds between departments and subject—not just simple arithmetic. Needs of different subjects must be assessed and given adequate ' weighting '. The ' half life ' of books and periodicals varies considerably from subject to subject. Some disciplines rely more heavily than others on expensive primary source materials. Whilst science and technology is currently thought to have prior claim on funds it should be remembered in the library that basic scientific equipment— electron microscopes, computers etc are financed out of special funds. Basic equipment for an English faculty might be thought of as being a collection of autograph letters or a first folio, and these are a call on library funds. Library fund requirements of non-technical departments should not, therefore, be submerged beneath current insistence on technical development.

44

Allocation of funds also depends upon the teaching practices and methods in departments. Programmes primarily lecture-based usually require students to have access to a small number of basic texts which they are expected to buy. Many industrial trainees at technical colleges are able to reclaim costs of texts from their employers. Where this happens, calls on library funds for basic texts are materially reduced. When courses are tutorial-based, requirement is for a wide range of material rather than heavy duplication of basic texts. Amount of research, or possibilities of developing useful research projects in particular subjects, will also need to be taken into account in planning allocations.

The effective deployment of resources will also need to take account of number of separate service points in the library. Overheads will be greater if more than one. For example, basic reference books and bibliographies will need to be duplicated. Possibilities of useful co-operation with local public and special libraries need to be explored on a subject by subject basis. But any tendency of academic librarians to rely upon the public libraries to duplicate text books for undergraduate provision is not appreciated by public librarians. This is especially true where access to the research collections at the university are denied to public library users.

INTERNAL ORGANISATION OF BOOK SELECTION

Practice varies from libraries where teaching staff play major part in selection to those in which librarian is totally responsible for purchasing. In many European universities book selection is entirely a library responsibility. In Britain and America practice is for some degree of joint consultation between library and teaching staff. Teaching staff are considered the final arbiters of quality but the librarian watches balance of stock, corrects any bias which might arise in teaching staff selection policy and supplements these activities with purchases of reference books and bibliographies. Librarian's task is the near impossible reconciliation of faculty demands with funds available. In some cases he must select materials on behalf of tax departments or individuals.

In those European countries where the library is an autonomous unit, selection of materials is carried out by subject specialists who are also librarians—perhaps the ideal solution but only if funds available are adequate to allow them full scope and if they are in constant touch with the teaching requirements of their subject. Wilson and Tauber (in their *University libraries*) note that this subject specialist/librarian approach as it is applied in New York Public Library results in the selection of a greater number of titles which later emerge as standard works than does the usual academic library librarian/teaching staff specialist approach.

Teaching staff members naturally select more with their own immediate needs in mind than for the total good of the institution. They can hardly be expected to be aware of the broader philosophies which impel the librarian. The librarian's role in this situation is to provide both the guidance for the initial selection impetus and judgment of the final balance to be struck. Complete success in this role is hard to achieve and only a strong, positive personality is likely to get anywhere near it.

Good writings on the subject of academic library book selection are few. The development of adequate definitions of scope, purposes and functions are singularly lacking. However, there is growing recognition that solutions must be sought. The core of the book selection problem in academic and in other types of libraries is that of discerning the true functions of the institution itself. J H P Pafford's article in UNESCO *Bulletin* (see above) is the most important recent writing and can be supplemented by L S Thompson's questioning article ' The Dogma of book selection in university libraries ' *Colleges and research libraries* 21 (6) November 1960 441-445. Thompson's article is a probe into the core of the problem and he exposes many issues worthy of considered examination. His central argument that exhaustive collection within clearly defined, if limited, subject areas results in a more effective total collection than miscellaneous selection on a basis of individual decisions, is most interestingly developed. ' Book selection and book stock ' by B C Bloomfield *Education libraries bulletin* (20) Summer 1964 1-18, examines the problem of selection for many college libraries. Selection on a basis of individual decisions is interestingly developed.

SPECIAL COLLECTIONS
Obtained by either purchase or donation. Collections of note are most likely to be attracted to libraries with an established reputation. A library would be morally wrong to accept donation of a

collection simply as an embellishment without any particular purpose—there should be academic justification sufficient to ensure that collection will be well used. Where collection is considered for purchase same pre-condition applies. In both cases funds to maintain and develop collection must be available.

Other circumstances affect the decision whether or not to accept an offered collection. Will it require any special accommodation or storage? Can these be provided without effect upon other resources? Will the expenses of reception and processing be repaid by use? Are there any limiting factors or conditions upon the use or disposition of the collection? Do the vendors insist it be kept together or can it be integrated into stock. Sometimes conditions are attached to the use of collections of little or no special merit. Particularly awkward are collections of no total merit but with a few items of great value or utility to a particular library. If it is a condition of sale that collection of this nature be preserved in totality, then the librarian is faced with unpleasant decisions. Collections should, ideally, be offered free of conditions except in cases of special merit.

STANDARDS OF STOCK

Many statements exist of minimum size of collections, ' ideal ' book funds, levels of expenditure and so on. All must be approached with caution for they usually take no account of existing collections, their size, nature or quality. Standards which specify expenditure of so many shillings per student for book fund are unhelpful if no regard is paid to fact that small student body does not mean that a less diversified stock is needed.

Standards which provide basis for development of a well established library may be totally inadequate for a new library. Recommended minimum standards can be a two edged weapon, they may be a goad to the backward but can also be an embarrassment to the progressive.

While not mentioning standards of stock specifically J Thompson ' University libraries and higher education ' *Library Association record* 66 (11) 1964 466-471 exposes the unreality of thinking of minima in a country where basic adequacy is often the criterion of the better libraries. Only comparisons with other countries have any meaning. While it is easy to shrug off direct comparisons of British and American libraries on the basis of relative economic

47

strengths, it is less easy to account for fact of swifter growth rates in some commonwealth and European countries.

Although it should be pointed out that there are a number of series of minimum standards in existence for various types of academic libraries, notably those issued by the AUT and the LA, it should also be said that in practice they have sometimes proved so inadequate as to be a barrier to progressive thinking.

There is not, and never can be, an adequate basis for computing minimum stock standards. The only standard a library has is that of the largest amount which can be obtained by an imaginative, resourceful librarian, and which can be effectively and economically disbursed within a particular pattern of organisation. It is a great source of fascination (and occasionally of frustration) in librarianship to appreciate that stock building objectives change as the library grows. A plan which is intended to raise the quality of a collection hardly ever succeeds in satisfying either the librarian or library users, since the attainment of an objective only reveals further, if distant, objectives.

CHAPTER SIX: SPECIAL DEPARTMENTS AND COLLECTIONS

MERGERS and takeovers in industry and commerce take place, amongst other things, to reap the benefits of economies of scale of production. By introducing specialised handling and production methods and by creating specialised staff units, a higher production from two or more merged units is looked for than the sum of the firms' previous, separate efforts. In library terms the converse of this argument can be applied. For administrative purposes staff can be used more economically if there is only one large unit to be administered. The price of fragmentation into smaller units is, inevitably, that more staff are needed, probably more accommodation and certainly a greater amount of administrative overheads. The reward is, or should be, greater effectiveness of reader service and more satisfaction in staff, due to their having a more interesting and amenable function to perform.

The increase in staff, accommodation etc arises from the need to provide an irreducible minimum of staff for reader service at all times the library is open. However, it also occurs because the very fact of dividing a stock into more specialised elements makes it easier to see where developments are needed and simplifies putting them into effect. The demands of users also become more insistent as the library improves its service—a good specialised library often meets more criticism than a poor general library simply because users expect more of it.

NATIONAL LIBRARIES

Tend to be divided by physical form of the material *eg* printed books, mss, maps, music (BM National Libraries of Scotland, Wales and Austria). This makes subject approach difficult, as does also the tendency for national libraries to be unclassified or to have many special collections which are kept together in remote parts of the library and inaccessible to users.

Division on a subject basis is practised by some libraries either totally as in the L of C and the National Diet Library Tokyo, or partially as in the Lenin Library.

The symposium on national libraries in Europe in 1958 came out strongly in favour of a measure of decentralisation within the national library, while rejecting the possibility of hiving off responsibility for the provision of national library type services by a number of special libraries on a subject basis. Division by subject is important to ensure that the best use is made of the rapidly increasing stocks of national libraries, especially in scientific and technical fields. The role of the national library in these fields was discussed by Quincey Mumford in his paper to the Asian regional seminar in UNESCO *Bulletin*.

ACADEMIC LIBRARIES

Whether demands of departments and divisions within the university or college for their own specialised libraries should be acceded to is the largest single unresolved issue in the academic libraries. P Havard-Williams in an article ' The Modern university library ' UNESCO *Bulletin* 13 (5-6) May-June 1959 110-114 states that these demands are a criticism of the main library. This is rather sweeping. The need for staff and students engaged upon research is for their most immediate research materials to be close to hand and easily accessible. The increasing size of university campuses, and the number of detached units located some distance away from the central campus, make the creation of departmental libraries desirable and, however much it may be deplored on administrative grounds by the librarian, it is often necessary in order to provide effective service. Another reason for its introduction may be problems of space occurring in the main library.

Within academic libraries departmental libraries function in one of several ways:

1 As entirely separate entities having no connection with the main university library.

2 Operating as detached arms of the main library, with university library personnel, and enjoying the benefits of main library administrative and technical services.

3 Operating within the framework of the main library but carrying out all administrative and technical services within the department.

50

The first method is extensively practised on the continent of Europe where such separate libraries are commonly called institute libraries. Robert Vosper 'European university libraries . . .' issue of *Library trends* 12 (4) April 1964 reiterates the difficulties engendered by this mode of organisation in Spain, Italy, Scandinavia, Austria, Great Britain and other countries examined. It is uneconomic on grounds of staffing, acquisition and use of space. It produces a greater tendency to duplicate and to ignore the benefits of the collections of the central library than do the other modes of decentralisation, where lack of appreciation of the importance of the bibliographical services and provision of materials peripheral to departmental collections are still a danger. H Tveteras in 'The University library and the institute libraries' *Libri* 9 (1) 1959 1-8, describes the methods used in Norway to overcome the principal difficulties in bringing the previously independent institute libraries more into the ambit of the main library. Rightly, he stresses need for main library staff to adopt positive attitudes to service to departments and by so doing prove beyond doubt that professional competence coupled with academic distinction in library staff provides better service to users than does a completely independent departmental collection. Provision of a better service to departments rather than the administrative convenience of the main library is, however, the crux of the matter.

The second method, that of operating as detached arms of the main library, is a compromise often practised. It allows for some central control of acquisitions, ensuring that expensive general reference material is not being provided in too many places or that excessive duplication of certain books or periodicals is not occurring. The main library's control of staff assists in ensuring that services of main library are appreciated at departmental level, since some transfer of staff between departments and the main library—especially at the junior level—can act as liaison for the main library's services. Specialist services of cataloguers and the administrative economies in providing central clerical and manual services are enjoyed, freeing departmentally based staff to perform effectively their true functions of reader service.

The third method, whereby many administrative and clerical services are carried out at departmental level is sometimes necessary when the departmental work is so specialised—maps, music, rare books, manuscripts etc—that only specialists can handle it effectively. It is also employed if the departmental library is, besides being specialised, large enough to form a complete and self-supporting entity *eg* certain University of London libraries or the Manchester College of Science and Technology.

It should be appreciated that local conditions may dictate that these modes of departmental service exist in combination within a given institution. The incredibly complex networks of London University and its colleges and of Harvard, Cambridge and Oxford Universities are cases in point.

A further structure might also be superimposed on the whole in the especially large universities whereby the main library is organised on a subject divisional plan. The principal advantage of this plan, compared with departmental libraries, is that, while retaining the benefits of specialist library staff advice, peripheral and wide ranging enquiries do not need to use collections in several different locations. The general reference and bibliographical collections can be used to greater advantage. In a tightly knit campus this plan works especially well. The whole problem of departmental and divisional libraries is brilliantly examined by David W Heron in ' The Centrifugence of university libraries ' *College and research libraries* 23 (3) May 1962 223-226.

THE UNDERGRADUATE COLLECTION
Whether or not a separate library service specifically geared to the curriculum needs of undergraduates should be provided is yet another major unresolved question in academic administration.

Advocates of separate provision maintain that the size of the main library tends to overwhelm, and the relative difficulty in locating materials appropriate to undergraduate needs induces ' anti-library ' reactions in students. It is argued that to provide a separate library with special staff improves library ' image ' with students and removes strain from the main library, allowing it to concentrate more effectively on service at graduate level.

Opponents argue that to ' pre-digest ' reading material by a separate, relatively low level provision does nothing to impress the good student with the ' power ' of a large library or give him the incentive to delve deeply or range widely in his chosen subject field.

B S Page in his paper ' University library development ' LA *Proceedings of the annual conference 1957 pp 52-57* refers to the need for a reference service to students administered by what he calls a 'student consultant'. His further point that undergraduates need to be encouraged to read widely for recreation as well as for instruction is often catered for by special undergraduate collections. W B Kuhn's article 'Princeton's New Julian Street Library' *College and research libraries* 23 (6) November 1962 504-508 describes how this is accomplished in one university. The 'house libraries' at Harvard and, to a lesser extent, the college libraries at Oxford and Cambridge illustrate the same principle in operation.

One consideration in providing separate collections is that they enable multiple copies of essential textbooks to be more effectively administered. T H Bowyer in his article 'Considerations on book provision for undergraduates in British university libraries' *Journal of documentation* 19 (4) December 1963 151-167, and the AUT survey *The University library* (AUT 1964) both make the point that undergraduates do not buy as many of their essential texts as they should. Even if they can be encouraged or obliged to buy more, the problem still remains of books needed only for a short time during studies of minor aspects of syllabuses. It is here that the undergraduate collection can help, as can a university bookshop with a trade in secondhand texts. A contribution can also be made by the provision of a text book rental service run on commercial lines. Some universities feel this type of service to be sufficiently essential to deserve a subsidy. In some American universities rental collections are run by a student/staff committee. While, usually, independent of the library, they contribute significantly to the solution of one of the library's most pressing problems.

It hardly needs saying that where an undergraduate library exists, no barriers should be placed in the way of a student wishing to use the main library. A summary of the case for separate undergraduate provision is made by F H Wagman in 'Library service to undergraduate college students' *College and research libraries* 17 (2) March-April 1956 143-148.

SPECIAL COLLECTIONS
Take several forms—collections of material physically different from the main stock *eg* maps, music, manuscripts etc, seminar and laboratory collections and collections bought, donated or bequested as separate entities. Some libraries appoint someone to assume overall charge of special collections.

First category—physically different materials and materials requiring special treatment in storage, cataloguing or use—is dealt with by Frances J Brewer in her article 'Special problems of special collections' *College and research libraries* 23 (3) May 1962. The conflict here is between the need for special treatment and the desirability of such materials being divided by subject to make them more accessible to users in divisional and departmental libraries. Special equipment for storage and expertise for administration is, however, most effectively and economically supplied by dealing with these special forms individually and centrally.

Second category—seminar libraries—are only finely divided from departmental libraries. They might be categorised as workshop collections in laboratories, classrooms and teaching staff rooms with no librarian in charge of them. In some colleges such collections are regarded as basic equipment and paid for out of departmental funds, thus placing them outside the library preview. It is not uncommon, of course, for such seminar libraries to develop into departmental libraries proper. Wilson and Tauber discuss the organisation and administration of these collections and their use in *The University library*.

Collections bought, donated and bequested and preserved as separate entities are discussed in chapter five.

CHAPTER SEVEN
TEACHING AND RESEARCH

INCREASING enrolments, drives to improve quality, greater numbers of post-graduate research students, larger staffs, all indicate the need for improved library services. A pronounced trend in university teaching is towards private reading, tutorials and ' self-organisation ' as Fulton *Experiment in higher education* (Tavistock Institute) shows. James F Govan ' This is, indeed, the heart of the matter ' *College and research libraries* 23 (6) November 1962 467-472, emphasises that the librarian's role in education is dynamic and thrusting. Such is the increase in the amount of literature produced that the librarian must think of himself much more as the guide to, rather than the guardian of, knowledge.

To comprehend the attitudes and objectives of research, librarians need to understand the nature of the problems faced by research workers. One way of doing this is for the librarian himself to be capable of research effort. Given the present structure of university and national library staffing, such research effort must be carried out before taking up senior appointments in libraries. Should not librarians be given opportunities to develop or continue research programmes? Is sabbatical leave at regular intervals the answer? Should library personnel be encouraged to obtain secondment to teaching posts for short periods? A M McAnally in his article ' Social pressures and academic librarianship ' ALA *Bulletin* 56 (2) February 1962 159-164 claims that librarians are indeed, ignorant of the methods and goals of education and lack intellectual stature in specialised fields. If this be so how can mutually respectful librarian/researcher relations be maintained? McAnally is not alone in claiming that librarians need to do more research. W S Dix refers to the same problem in ' Leadership in academic libraries ' *College and research libraries* 21 (5) September 1960 373-380.

Writers on academic library themes in the American library press are preoccupied with questions of status. As in technical college and training college libraries in Britain, many librarians have not achieved equality with teaching staff in American academic libraries. Their lack of academic stature is a frequently cited reason for this situation. D P Bergen in ' Librarians and the bipolarisation of the academic enterprise' *College and research libraries* 24 (6) November 1963 467-480 feels that there is a lack of rapport between librarians and teaching staffs which is reaching serious proportions. His tendency to place the bulk of the blame on the shoulders of the librarian will not be popular. He claims that librarians, through their preoccupation with the technical and administrative aspects of their work, are becoming incapable of making objective assessments of their role in the promotion of research. He sees the frequent conflict between teaching staff and librarians, over the desirability or otherwise of allowing for the creation of departmental libraries, as a symptom of this and concludes that it is the librarian who must concede ground in this argument if educational objectives are to be properly attained.

SUBJECT SPECIALISATION BY LIBRARIANS
Relations between the librarian and the library user need to be mutually respectful. Neither party should feel obliged to pay lip service to the other's importance. Bergen (*ibid*) and R S Smith ' The Special library in the university' in *The Two cultures* (LA Reference, special and information section conference papers 1961) both note the need for more librarian/specialists with a knowledge of how research proceeds. The specialist is not required to assist the researcher directly from his own knowledge. It would not be possible to provide enough specialists to do this even if it were desirable. It is simply that a person versed in research techniques finds it easier to make the mental adjustment to the needs of the researcher with the appropriate depth of thought than would a person not so versed.

Librarian/specialists can make a significant contribution to research and teaching effort at departmental level. Librarian/user relations can be more intensively developed. Users come to know the librarian intimately and can develop confidence in his ability —a most important factor. Weak staff members can more easily be recognised under such conditions; a passenger whose incompetence might not be fully appreciated in a centralised library soon becomes apparent under a departmental structure.

That librarians are coming to grips with the issues involved in relations with users is obvious from the large number of user surveys being carried out. N N Nicholson and E Bartlett 'Who uses university libraries?' *College and research libraries* 22 (3) May 1962 217-222 gives an example of a library user questionnaire. Important to realise that every institution poses special problems —physical location of the library, modes of teaching, personalities of teaching staffs, researchers and librarians, scope, size and depth of the library stock all affect particular local situations. Reports of surveys in other libraries, although interesting, are no substitute for an individual assessment. A number of recent surveys do allow certain general conclusions to be reached which have a bearing on all aspects of academic library policy, especially building and selection. Great need is for hours of opening to be extended and a greater degree of direct reference service provided. Constant pressure for creation of departmental libraries is frequently expressed by contributors to such surveys. First degree students call for greater duplication of basic texts. Should be remembered, however, that the AUT survey *The University library* asserts that students must buy more books themselves. Questions regarding students' book buying habits should be included in questionnaires.

Recent reports of surveys can be read with profit: A N Oppenheim 'The Reading habits of students' *Journal of documentation* 18 (2) June 1962; M B Line 'Student attitudes to the university library' *Journal of documentation* 19 (3) September 1963 100-117; P H Taylor 'A Survey of library use by second year students at a training college for teachers' *Education libraries bulletin* 7 (Spring) 1960 5-16; 'What they read: notes on two recent readership surveys' *Library Association record* 66 (5) May 1964 207-8. This reports surveys at Bolton and Northampton Technical Colleges.

NATIONAL LIBRARIES

Scope of services to readers varies according to degree of departmentalisation, or lack of it. In many countries the national library is a 'last resort' collection available only to researchers able to prove their needs. In some countries however, the national library serves also as a university library (*eg* Scandinavia) or even as a home reading library also (India, Singapore). Generally speaking, Asian national libraries have not yet become completely the province of the researcher.

Probably the point at which the national library enjoys the closest relationship with its users is in the provision of a legislative reference service. An article by J O Wilson is included in the reports of the seminar on the development of national libraries in Asia and the Pacific area in UNESCO *Bulletin*.

TRAINING IN LIBRARY USE

That so much has been written in recent years about the need to provide extensive guidance in the use of libraries for students is probably proof enough that this most basic of requirements is not adequately covered at present. In national libraries guidance is principally carried out by the production of a handbook which describes collections and services available. A limited amount of reader assistance is usually offered in the reading room. Examples of handbooks are the British Museum *A Guide to the public services,* the National Library of Wales *A Brief summary of its history and activities* and the Library of Congress *Information for readers in the Library of Congress.* Guided tours provided, for example, by the British Museum are hardly adequate introductions for researchers.

In academic libraries emphasis in assistance is upon the provision of courses (though this is frequently a euphuism for a guided tour) for freshmen. Of equal importance is provision of courses for senior undergraduate and graduate students—even for staff members. O M V Argles ' The Work of the tutor librarian ' *Library world* 63 (744) June 1962 314-317 and N Burgess ' G courses and the library ' *Technical journal* 1 (7) October 1963 11, 13 describe such courses. R E McCoy 'Automation in freshman library instruction ' *Wilson library bulletin* 36 (6) February 1962 468-470, 472 introduces concept of using teaching machines for such work. See also E G Holley and R W Oram ' University library orientation by television ' *College and research libraries* 23 (6) November 1962 485-491. P Havard-Williams and L H Davey provide a survey of the Australasian approach in their article ' Reader instruction in commonwealth university libraries ' *Library Association record* 62 (1) January 1960 10-13.

Readers' handbooks are also issued by many academic libraries.

Less usual is a special handbook issued for staff members. R M Lightfoot examines the need for such a handbook in his 'On issuing a faculty library handbook' *Wilson library bulletin* 36 (3) November 1961 234-236. This gives advice on writing and a specimen of contents.

REFERENCE SERVICE IN ACADEMIC LIBRARIES

The old adage that service is on three levels in academic libraries dies hard in the textbooks. No longer is it true to say that all academic libraries provide a reference and enquiry service only to teaching staff, give only bibliographical advice to post-graduates and virtually no help at all to undergraduates. That some libraries still operate in this way is more a rationalisation of their staffing inadequacies than a conviction that this is the best way to provide academic library service. The AUT survey calls for the development of reference services with, however, the very important reminder that it is not the function of the library to do other people's research. The survey points out that the library has a responsibility to provide staff members and other researchers with information about new bibliographical developments in their fields. Again, the fact that this needs to be pointed out indicates that at the moment it is not being done effectively enough.

RECREATIONAL COLLECTIONS

Should academic libraries dilute the impact of their basic functions by providing recreational literature? Such service is expensive and time consuming. Would such service assist in improving library/user relations? Is it part of the true function of the academic library to provide for the broader development of its users—especially with the introduction of liberal studies courses into the curricula of further education institutions and of more broadly based courses in some universities?

There is scope for co-operation with the local public libraries —county mobile libraries call at many college campuses and at such institutions as the NLL. New campuses offer scope for the incorporation of part or full time branches of public libraries on or near their campuses. Some academic libraries provide rental collections from a subscription library for recreational purposes. Occasionally the staff common-room committee or students' union pay for the facility. Library often acts as the administrative vehicle in this case.

USE BY OUTSIDERS

Because of pressure on their collections national and academic libraries, in the western world at least, are traditionally reserved for the use of the advanced researcher (in the case of national libraries) and for accredited members (in the case of academic libraries). Because both are supported substantially from community funds it is sometimes argued that they have no right to restrict entry. The difficulties that providing unrestricted entry for all comers would create are too self evident to need comment —the number of status seeking pseudo scholars who would wish to use the British Museum would be more than sufficient to disrupt the service. This is not to say that national libraries should be given complete protection from the demands of outside users. In the UK a greater degree of integration into the national system of libraries would be of great benefit. Many academic libraries are on rather difficult ground if they try to restrict access, since they enjoy privileges of the library licence agreement under which they undertake to allow access to outsiders upon demand.

At least a part of the troubles of accommodation caused in national libraries are due to the short hours of opening. Return on capital invested in them, if it could be measured, would probably be found to be alarmingly small. Longer opening hours and a degree of participation in inter library co-operation would improve the return.

Many technical college libraries issue bulletins and documentation surveys to teaching staff and others—this reflects a generally more positive attitude to reader service, compared with university libraries (HERTIS and Bradford Institute of Technology are examples). Their willingness to co-operate in schemes like TALIC and NANTIS are another indication (see chapter eight).

CHAPTER EIGHT: CO-OPERATION

AN important aspect of co-operation affecting all research libraries has been the various schemes developed to systematise the collection of foreign literature. National libraries can no longer claim to attempt to be totally comprehensive, not even the largest of them, even if such a claim was ever realistic. National libraries all need to limit their coverage to a greater or lesser extent—the BM limits itself to the humanities in the collection of foreign literature. Even the great Library of Congress has had to acknowledge the inevitable. The National Libraries of Agriculture and of Medicine and the existence of the *National union catalog* are signs of this.

Schemes of co-operative acquisition have, therefore, been introduced in many countries to ensure that some semblance of comprehensiveness in foreign literature is obtained on a national basis. Three most important schemes of this nature are the Farmington Plan, the Scandia Plan and the scheme operated through the Deutsche Forschungsgemeinschaft. Schemes of subject specialisation operated by some countries in an attempt to provide comprehensive coverage of a nation's own publications are significant support for a foreign literature acquisition scheme, since they take some of the load off the national library. The Dutch Royal and National Library, for example, concentrates its efforts on acquiring foreign literature, relying upon the national co-operative acquisition scheme to provide coverage of Dutch material.

The introduction of these schemes, and other enterprises of a more limited nature, such as the ' background scheme ' for early British books, implies that a high degree of goodwill and mutual trust exists between libraries of, sometimes, very different character and purpose. Such good relations need to exist on an international as well as an intra-national plane and national and academic libraries have a particularly good record in this respect.

In 1958 a symposium on national libraries in Europe was held in Vienna. The papers and resulting recommendations appear in

National libraries, their problems and prospects (UNESCO 1960), and a summary of the main points was published in *Libri* 9 (4) 1959 273-307. A regional seminar on the development of national libraries in Asia and the Pacific area was held in Manila in February 1964; some of the papers and conclusions arising appeared in UNESCO *Bulletin* 18 (4) July-August 1964. Meetings of this sort are important as a means of creating an atmosphere of interdependence and for sharing experience and problems. Both were promoted under UNESCO auspices.

The International Federation of Library Associations' section, the International Association of Technical University Libraries, established in 1955 is a useful link and publishes IATUL *Newsletter*. In 1952 a National and Universities section of IFLA came into being. Nationally, research libraries frequently have special bodies to represent them, for example the Association of Research Libraries in the United States, SCONUL (Standing Conference of National and University Libraries) and the Scandinavian Association of Research Libraries. There are special sections of many national associations of librarians, for example, the University and Research section of the Library Association and the Association of College and Research Libraries division of the American Library Association.

SCONUL

Detailed reviews of activities by K W Humphreys in *Libri* 7 (1) 1956 41-44 and 12 (1) 1962 56-60.

SCONUL was founded in 1950 ' to promote work of national and universities libraries '. It does this by regular meetings of representatives of large learned libraries, besides the national libraries (including National Library of Ireland), NCL, NLL, Patent Office, Science Museum, BM (Natural History), Public Record Office and the John Rylands Library, and librarians of all British universities and of several major colleges, chiefly of London University, are represented.

There are a number of special committees in addition to the executive committee. One of these, the Co-operation in Acquisitions committee, is of particular relevance here. This committee has examined the possibilities of operating a ' Farmington Plan ' in the United Kingdom and has surveyed coverage of a number of types of foreign material in British libraries, history periodicals, classics and medicine periodicals, Russian periodicals in cover to cover translation, and a survey of holdings of American literature (see B R Crick 'A Survey of library resources in the United Kingdom for the teaching of American history in the Universities' *Journal of documentation* 14 (2) 1958 109).

The Association of Research Libraries came into being in 1931 with the object of developing and increasing the usefulness of research collections in American libraries.

The Scandinavian Association of Research Libraries includes individual and corporate members from all Scandinavian countries. It was described in UNESCO *Bulletin* 12 (12) November-December 1958 296.

Of the specialist sections of the LA and the ALA, the LA University and Research section came into being in 1928 and has sub-sections for colleges of technology and further education and for education and teacher training college libraries. The ACRL was founded in 1889 and works through fifteen committees. Its official organ is the bi-monthly *College and research libraries*.

CO-OPERATIVE ACQUISITION—THE BACKGROUND SCHEME
Developed by the Joint Standing Committee on Library Co-operation of the Association of University Teachers. The scheme has the aim of dividing up the field of acquisition of retrospective material into units of ten years. Each participating library is allocated a period in which to purchase material as it becomes available. The period up to 1800 AD is covered. The organisation of the scheme is described in *British universities annual 1964* (AUT).

THE FARMINGTON PLAN
Established in 1948, named after town in Connecticut where preliminary discussions were held in 1942. Administered by the Association of Research Libraries. Aim is to improve the flow of foreign language materials into the United States. To this end a number of large American research libraries have agreed to accept responsibility for taking significant book and pamphlet materials on either a subject basis or, in some cases, a country basis. The country basis is used to deal with languages which few American libraries are prepared to handle and for countries in which the book trade is poorly organised. In most cases assignments of subjects are to libraries which already have strong, relevant collections.

63

Acquisition of materials is effected by the appointment of agents —usually leading booksellers—who are advised by librarians to select and forward the most significant items published in their country to the library to whom the subject is assigned. These agencies are appointed by the ARL in most instances, but since 1959 libraries have been able to appoint their own agents if they so wish.

The Vosper-Talmadge report of 1959 (official title *Farmington Plan survey: final report* published by ARL) was a most significant event. Previously only Western Europe had been well covered and the report resulted in a much expanded programme coming into operation. Material acquired is quickly reported to the *National union catalog* and made available for inter library loan. Readings are *Farmington plan handbook 1953*, not entirely superseded by the second edition published in 1961 which contains a summary of the Vosper-Talmadge report. Dr Vosper's ' Farmington redivivus ' *Aslib proceedings* 11 (11) November 1959 327-334 is also useful.

SCANDIA PLAN

Besides a section ' Co-operative acquisition: what is being done in Scandinavia ' in *National libraries: their problems and prospects* (UNESCO 1960) 89-96 by H L Tveteras, there is an article in *Libri* 9 (1) 1959 1-8 also by Tveteras and T Kleberg's ' Some notes on the Scandia Plan ' *Libri* 12 (1) 1962 76-84.

The plan is similar to Farmington and had its genesis in the scheme developed by four major Swedish research libraries in 1955 to co-operate in the acquisition of foreign material. In 1956 a start was made in extending the scheme to cover the whole of Scandinavia. Based on the known subject and linguistic interests of libraries, it began by concentrating upon the humanities, later spreading to other fields. An important by product has been the improved relations enjoyed by libraries of similar type in the different countries—the parliamentary libraries, for example, have begun a scheme of their own for the collection of parliamentary papers.

DEUTSCHE FORSCHUNGSGEMEINSCHAFT CO-OPERATIVE PROCUREMENT SCHEME

Besides acting as a central clearing house for national and international exchanges and for inter library co-operation, the DFG seeks to improve the availability of foreign scientific literature throughout Western Germany.

A plan has been devised whereby the larger German libraries have been assigned a ' special collection field ' and given funds to enable them to purchase the most important foreign books and periodicals published since 1939 (or in some cases 1930). At the same time the library is expected to acquire native material in the ' field ', intensively. Books obtained under the scheme are selected at the library's own discretion, but periodicals are purchased in accordance with a set plan. Inter library co-operation is developed out of this basic plan and support given to the creation of union catalogues on a regional basis and to union lists of periodicals and indexes to periodical literature.

A pamphlet *German Research Association: structure and functions* is available freely from DFG, Frankgengraben 40, Bad Godesburg, West Germany. L S Thompson ' Subject specialisation in German research libraries ' is contained in the Vosper-Talmadge report.

CO-OPERATIVE STORAGE AND STORAGE LIBRARIES
This can take the form of several libraries combining to purchase a cheap, accessible storage area for the storage of little used materials, with facilities for its swift return when required, the ownership of the materials remaining strictly with the storing library. Alternatively the co-operatively acquired store can be administered as a cohesive whole with the materials sent to the store being collated into one sequence and duplicates either returned to individual libraries or disposed of. Title in the material stored becomes vested in the co-operating libraries jointly and each library can call on material irrespective of previous ownership: In some systems the store also acts as a purchasing agent, collecting further background materials and buying to complete or extend existing holdings.

A further method is for a group of libraries to agree to receive material from each other in particular subject fields and to sort it into their own storage files, returning or disposing of duplicates. The law libraries of London University co-operate in this way.

Whichever method is adopted the purpose is the same—to alleviate pressure on storage areas in co-operating libraries unable, or unwilling, to extend stores on existing sites. A number of the constituent libraries of London University share a store at Egham in Surrey to which they send little used material. A similar arrangement is operated by the New England Deposit Library.

The Mid West Inter Library Center (MILC) is perhaps the best known co-operative store. While allowing libraries wishing to retain title in their own material to rent space MILC is essentially an organisation designed to collate material sent to it and to retain one copy at least, disposing of the surplus if the donating library consents. The scheme enables great economy to be made in the storage of little used material.

Articles describing the activities of MILC and other storage schemes are H J Harrar ' Co-operative storage warehouses' *College and research libraries* 25 (1) January 1964 37-43, and Jerrold Orne ' Storage and deposit libraries' *College and research libraries* 21 (6) November 1960 446-452. The first describes MILC, HILC and the New England Deposit Library, the second discusses the philosophy behind such libraries and questions the values in book selection which make them necessary.

NATIONAL LENDING LIBRARY FOR SCIENCE AND TECHNOLOGY

Though not to be viewed strictly as a storage library (it is more truly a national specialised library in its own right) the NLL does display some of the functions of a co-operative store. Through its acceptance of significant files of little used periodicals for permanent storage it ensures the retention of material in such a way that it can be re-borrowed, subject to need. Files are also, thereby, made more easily available to other libraries than if they were kept in a library not geared to nation wide lending techniques.

The NLL function of collecting as wide a spread as possible of the world's technical literature can solve many of the selection problems of other libraries. The knowledge that ' fringe' and secondary materials can freely and easily be obtained—in translation if required—enables the individual library to concentrate its resources upon its primary needs and, more important, to devote more attention to building up first class bibliographical services.

THE NATIONAL LIBRARY IN CO-OPERATION

In many countries the national library is the centre of all bibliographic activity and library endeavour. In the more advanced countries where an empiric build-up of resources has taken place over a period of years, this concept sometimes does not hold good. Most do play some part in the leadership of library affairs but not all of them take a really substantial role. In the developing countries the shortage of facilities enables more closely integrated arrangements to be made for the development of libraries.

In planning the growth of a national structure of libraries in new and emergent countries since the second world war, the development of an adequate national library has frequently been seen as the first and most important step to be taken. It has been planned from the beginning as focus for the development of a library and bibliographical infra structure for the country.

The ideal concept of a country's library affairs has included the following points: that a bibliographic centre should be established at a very early stage and that the centre should be based upon the national library. The functions of the centre are described by Knud Larsen in *National bibliographical services* (UNESCO 1955).

The functions can be summarised as follows:

1 The establishment of a bibliographic information centre.

2 The production of a current national bibliography.

3 The creation of a national and international system of co-operation.

4 The creation of necessary union catalogues and the co-ordination of other bibliographical work.

5 Development of bibliographical and cataloguing standards for a country's libraries.

6 Co-ordination and development of retrospective national bibliography.

7 Encouragement and development of the training and professional grouping of librarians and bibliographers.

8 Production of select lists of books for the guidance of librarians in charge of newly created libraries.

9 Encouragement of the growth of an indigenous book trade.

10 Encouragement of the growth of research activity and availability of information on the scope and nature of research affecting the country, wherever it is undertaken.

Operation of such a range of activities as these, in addition to the roles traditionally ascribed to the national library, obviously helps to make it a very powerful force in the shaping of the librarianship affairs of a country. It is interesting—and a useful revision exercise—to try to isolate which of these ten points are carried out by the BM, BN and L of C, and which other bodies in Britain, France and America outside the national library structure deal with the rest.

OTHER CO-OPERATIVE ACTIVITIES OF NATIONAL LIBRARIES

Curt D Wormann comprehensively examines this in ' Co-operation of national libraries with other libraries in the same and in other countries' UNESCO *Bulletin* 18 (4) July-August 1964 165-171. F C Francis in ' The contribution of the national library to modern outlook in library services' ASLIB *Proceedings* 10 (11) November 1958 267-275 indicates how the BM is thinking about its role in the UK library system.

Some national libraries are the national clearing houses for national and international loans (this role was specifically abrogated by the BM in 1927 after a Kenyon Committee recommendation that they should take it on). Exchange of publications is also an activity for which many national libraries take responsibility. UNESCO has been active in promoting the flow of publications exchanges on an international basis, and has also assisted in the production of micro-recording projects designed to make available to the newer national libraries materials otherwise inaccessible. A most important non-UNESCO project in this field is one undertaken by the National Library of Ireland to obtain micro-records of materials of Irish interest held in the libraries of America, Britain and France.

ACADEMIC LIBRARIES

Besides some informal co-operation based upon known subject specialisations and upon union lists of periodicals, academic libraries play an important part in the formal machinery of co-operation. Existing published writings on co-operation, however, should be approached with the realisation that, despite the assumption they often make, formal co-operation does not simply mean the NCL regional library bureau systems and the interloan of books. However, the large number of new university, further education and training college library foundations do owe a considerable debt to such interloan schemes. The NLL has been a boon to the science and technology based libraries. Librarians of new academic libraries have frequently praised, in print, the way in which established libraries have assisted them both locally and nationally through the existing co-operative machinery.

There are a number of rough edges to be smoothed out in the relationship between public and academic libraries, notably the heavy demands made by undergraduates on text book materials in the public libraries. Whilst it can be argued that the public library should provide this material in proportion to the demand, the public librarian's suspicion that he is being used by the academic librarians as a means of avoiding their own responsibilities is not always without foundation. The students themselves, of course, seldom buy enough of their needs in basic textbooks.

Technical college libraries play an important role in such local schemes of co-operation as NANTIS (Nottingham and Nottinghamshire Technical Information Service) and TALIC (Tyneside Association of Libraries for Industry and Commerce). A number of colleges are bases for DSIR technical liaison centres. These organisations provide a link between colleges, industry and the research stations, assisting these with information problems in a very practical way. Many county and some county borough libraries have integrated their own technical library services with those of the technical colleges in their areas. Herts county, Nottinghamshire, Durham and Belfast city are examples.

Training colleges receive considerable assistance not only from their local institute of education libraries, which are available to college staffs for information and research, but also from local public libraries. The introduction of broadly based liberal studies programmes into many colleges opens up the possibility of even closer relationships between the libraries of the local authorities and the academies. The fact that, unlike the United States, most of the depositories of international and other official materials are public rather than academic libraries is another reason for close links between the two.

READING LIST

BOOKS

Esdaile, Arundel *National libraries of the world: their history, administration and public services* second edition revised by F J Hill, London, Library Association 1957

National libraries: their problems and prospects Paris, UNESCO 1960

The University library London, The Association of University Teachers 1964

Wilson, Louis R and Tauber, Maurice F *The University library: its organisation, administration and functions* first edition University of Chicago Press 1946, second edition University of Columbia Press 1956

PERIODICALS

College and research libraries the official journal of the Association of College and Research Libraries, a division of the American Library Association, published bi-monthly in January, March, May, July, September, November from 1,207 Bluff Street, Fulton, Missouri, USA (subscription orders handled at 50 East Huron Street, Chicago 11, USA)

Education libraries bulletin issued irregularly by the London University Institute of Education

Library literature a quarterly issued in March, June, September, December with bound annual and three year cumulated volumes, published by the H W Wilson Company, 950 University Avenue, Bronx, New York, USA

Library science abstracts published quarterly by the Library Association, Chaucer House, Malet Place, London WC1

Library trends published quarterly by the University of Illinois Press, Urbana, USA

UNESCO *Bulletin for libraries* published bi-monthly from 9 Place de Fontenoy, Paris 7e, France

Wilson library bulletin published every month from September to June by the H W Wilson Company

INDEX

73